STUDY GUIDE
UNSTUCK

Copyright © 2022 by Richard Perinchief

Published by AVAIL

All rights reserved. No portion of this book may be reproduced, stored in a retrieval system, or transmitted in any form or by any means—electronic, mechanical, photocopy, recording, scanning, or other—except for brief quotations in critical reviews or articles, without prior written permission of the author.

Scripture quotations marked NKJV are taken from the New King James Version®. Copyright © 1982 by Thomas Nelson. Used by permission. All rights reserved. | Scripture quotations marked NLT are taken from the Holy Bible, New Living Translation, copyright © 1996, 2004, 2015 by Tyndale House Foundation. Used by permission of Tyndale House Publishers, Inc., Carol Stream, Illinois 60188. All rights reserved. | Scripture quotations marked MSG are taken from THE MESSAGE, copyright © 1993, 1994, 1995, 1996, 2000, 2001, 2002 by Eugene H. Peterson. Used by permission of NavPress. All rights reserved. Represented by Tyndale House Publishers, Inc. | Scripture quotations marked TPT are from The Passion Translation®. Copyright © 2017, 2018 by Passion & Fire Ministries, Inc. Used by permission. All rights reserved. ThePassionTranslation.com.

For foreign and subsidiary rights, contact the author.

Cover design: Sara Young
Cover photo: Andrew van Tilborgh

ISBN: 978-1-957369-65-5   1 2 3 4 5 6 7 8 9 10

Printed in the United States of America

UN**STUCK**
STUDY GUIDE

Break Free.
Rise Up.
Launch Out.

RICHARD PERINCHIEF

CONTENTS

Introduction 6

Chapter 1. Stuck Happens 8

Chapter 2. Ditch Your Dead Moseses 14

Chapter 3. The Lies Hold Us Back 20

Chapter 4. Your Burning Bush Moment 24

Chapter 5. Show Your Scars 30

Chapter 6. Generations of Freedom 34

Chapter 7. Out of Your Control 38

Chapter 8. Where Are You? 42

Chapter 9. Supernatural, Not Superhuman 48

Chapter 10. Tune In 54

Chapter 11. Discerning His Voice 58

Chapter 12. That or Better 64

Chapter 13. Show Them How to Be Free 68

INTRODUCTION

Stuck isn't limited to pandemics, global financial crises, or personal life events that can feel crippling. . . . It can happen to non-Christians and Christians alike.

As you read the Introduction in *Unstuck*, review, reflect on, and respond to the text by answering the following questions.

REVIEW, REFLECT, AND RESPOND:

How can you tell when you are or another person is stuck?

_____
_____
_____
_____
_____
_____

How does that stuck-ness affect all parties involved?

_____
_____
_____
_____
_____
_____

What are you hoping to take away from *Unstuck*?

_____
_____
_____
_____
_____
_____

CHAPTER 1

STUCK HAPPENS

*As Christians, "stuck" can seem especially bad.
Aren't we expected to have the answers?*

As you read Chapter 1: "Stuck Happens" in *Unstuck*, review, reflect on, and respond to the text by answering the following questions.

REVIEW, REFLECT, AND RESPOND:

When have you felt stuck?

What did it feel like?

How did you get into that situation?

What counsel did others give you regarding your predicament?

> *We have become his poetry, a re-created people that will fulfill the destiny he has given each of us, for we are joined to Jesus, the Anointed One. Even before we were born, God planned in advance our destiny and the good works we would do to fulfill it!*
>
> —Ephesians 2:10 (TPT)

Consider the scripture above and answer the following questions:

How does your view of yourself compare to God's view of you—poetry, re-created, destined for good works?

_____
_____
_____
_____
_____

How far along are you on the path to your destiny? On what do you base your assessment?

_____
_____
_____
_____
_____

What good works has God planned in advance for you to do? Which have you accomplished successfully?

_____
_____
_____
_____
_____

How did you ultimately get unstuck?

Which parts of God's plan for your life are you having a hard time trusting?

How do you see His wisdom in giving you distinctive gifts and calling in those parts of your life?

What dashed hopes or broken dreams do you need to lay before God, so He can put them back together again?

_____
_____
_____
_____
_____
_____
_____

Respond to Pastor Richard's statement: "If you're still alive, it's not over." What hope can you draw from it?

_____
_____
_____
_____
_____
_____
_____

CHAPTER 2

DITCH YOUR DEAD MOSESES

God knows we're more likely to turn to Him when we're in trouble, and like a good Father, He is waiting for you when you're ready to ask Him some big questions.

As you read Chapter 2: "Ditch Your Dead Moseses" in *Unstuck*, review, reflect on, and respond to the text by answering the following questions.

REVIEW, REFLECT, AND RESPOND:

When do people commonly find themselves stuck?

_____
_____
_____
_____
_____
_____

To what lengths have you seen people go to get unstuck?

_____
_____
_____
_____
_____
_____

What provisions has God made to help people get unstuck?

_____
_____
_____
_____
_____
_____

> *All praises belong to the God and Father of our Lord Jesus Christ. For he is the Father of tender mercy and the God of endless comfort. He always comes alongside us to comfort us in every suffering so that we can come alongside those who are in any painful trial. We can bring them this same comfort that God has poured out upon us.*
>
> —2 Corinthians 1:3-4 (TPT)

Consider the scripture above and answer the following questions:

How have you seen the Father's tender mercy and endless comfort?

_____
_____
_____
_____
_____

What did it look like when He came alongside you?

_____
_____
_____
_____
_____

How did that strengthen you to come alongside someone else and give them comfort?

_____
_____
_____
_____
_____

Which of the below "big questions" have you found yourself asking when you've been stuck? What were some of their answers?

- Why am I here?
  _____
  _____
  _____
  _____

- Why did you make me like this?
  _____
  _____
  _____
  _____

- What am I supposed to do now?
  _____
  _____
  _____
  _____

- Am I willing to surrender to the opportunity before me so that God can speak into my life?

_____
_____
_____
_____

In what area of your life have you been trying to steer a parked car? What does that look like?

_____
_____
_____
_____
_____

What dead Moseses do you need to leave behind, so you can step into the blessings of your promised land?

_____
_____
_____
_____
_____

Why is it so hard to let go of what seems to be holding you back?

_____
_____
_____
_____
_____

What small steps can you take to get your car moving—even if it's just creeping—so you can arise and go?

_____
_____
_____
_____
_____
_____
_____

Think of someone you trust to assist you. What is your plan for enlisting that person's help?

_____
_____
_____
_____
_____
_____

CHAPTER 3

THE LIES HOLD US BACK

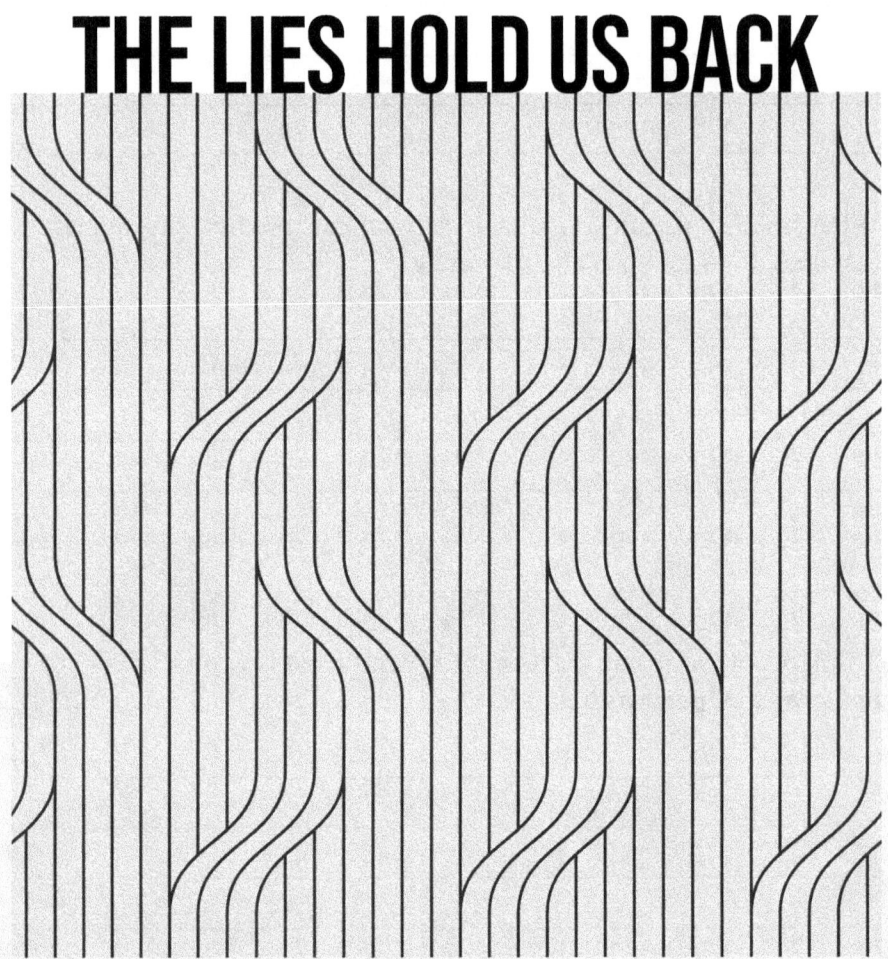

I know you're ready to be unstuck right now, but I need to bring something up: even though you may feel ready, God may need to begin a process in you.

As you read Chapter 3: "The Lies Hold Us Back" in *Unstuck*, review, reflect on, and respond to the text by answering the following questions.

REVIEW, REFLECT, AND RESPOND:

Pastor Richard shared a couple of names people use to refer to God: the Man upstairs, the Big Guy, etc. What words do you use to express your concept of God? Where did your concept of God come from?

_____
_____
_____
_____

In which "subjects" of your life is God the center? What does that look like?

_____
_____
_____
_____

Think of your current area of stuck-ness. How have you invited God's input and guidance into it?

_____
_____
_____
_____

How might your concept of God be hindering your ability to get unstuck?

_____
_____
_____

> *For we do not wrestle against flesh and blood, but against principalities, against powers, against the rulers of the darkness of this age, against spiritual hosts of wickedness in the heavenly places.*
>
> —*Ephesians 6:12 (NKJV)*

Consider the scripture above and answer the following questions:

Based on what you can see with your natural eyes, what "flesh and blood" are you wrestling against in order to get unstuck?

_____
_____
_____
_____
_____

How might Paul's revelation that you're really wrestling spiritual powers influence how you view your stuck-ness and the people who aren't helping you get unstuck?

_____
_____
_____
_____
_____

How can you reconcile the fact that the enemy uses even well-meaning people to do his work?

_____
_____
_____
_____

Per Pastor Richard's encouragement, ask: "God, what do You want to do in my life now?" What is He saying?

_____
_____
_____

How might God be positioning you for freedom as He works you through the process to get there? Think of the following areas:

- Preparing the ground of your heart

  _____
  _____
  _____

- Developing or growing something in you

  _____
  _____
  _____

- Showing you the sin He's clearing away

  _____
  _____
  _____

- Clarifying misunderstandings you have about Him or the Bible

  _____
  _____
  _____

- Making you aware of lies from the enemy that you've believed

  _____
  _____
  _____

CHAPTER 4

YOUR BURNING BUSH MOMENT

God has judged you, and He has found you worthy because of Jesus.

As you read Chapter 4: "Your Burning Bush Moment" in *Unstuck*, review, reflect on, and respond to the text by answering the following questions.

REVIEW, REFLECT, AND RESPOND:

How could a person actually impede the work of the Holy Spirit in their life?

_____
_____
_____
_____

What do the lifelines look like that people have thrown to you or others who were stuck?

_____
_____
_____
_____

What does it look like when people refuse to grab onto those lifelines?

_____
_____
_____
_____

What role does the spoken word play in a believer's life?

_____
_____
_____
_____

> *"Go back to John and tell him what you have heard and seen—the blind see, the lame walk, those with leprosy are cured, the deaf hear, the dead are raised to life, and the Good News is being preached to the poor."*
>
> —*Matthew 11:4-5 (NLT)*

Consider the scripture above and answer the following questions:

What crisis was John the Baptist facing?

How did John position himself to hear the answer to his big question?

How would Jesus' answer have encouraged John?

How have you seen a believer's spoken words—or someone else's—make or break the believer's faith?

_____
_____
_____
_____
_____
_____

How likely are you to compare yourself with other people? What does that look like? How does it feel?

_____
_____
_____
_____
_____
_____

What is your gut reaction to Pastor Richard's statement: "You don't have to make yourself into someone who is acceptable; you already are"?

_____
_____
_____
_____
_____
_____

Whose story from the Bible about God working with people right where they are gives you the most hope? Why?

_____
_____
_____
_____
_____
_____

What enemies does God want to destroy in your life? Comparison? Doubt? Fear?

_____
_____
_____
_____
_____
_____
_____

How would you encourage someone who doesn't know where to start in order for God to destroy those crippling agents of the enemy?

_____
_____
_____
_____
_____
_____

CHAPTER 5

SHOW YOUR SCARS

I say this to help answer a difficult question: if we're saved and set free, why does God let us get stuck?

As you read Chapter 5: "Show Your Scars" in *Unstuck*, review, reflect on, and respond to the text by answering the following questions.

REVIEW, REFLECT, AND RESPOND:

Think of someone—possibly yourself—who was stuck. Looking back at that situation, how do you see that it served a purpose either in that person's life or another's?

_____
_____
_____
_____
_____
_____

What risk do we run when we try to point out the purpose to another person's pain?

_____
_____
_____
_____
_____
_____
_____

Pastor Richard asked: If we're saved and set free, why does God let us get stuck? And what do we do about it? How would you answer?

_____
_____
_____
_____
_____
_____

> *Then [Jesus] said to Thomas, "Reach your finger here, and look at My hands; and reach your hand here, and put it into My side. Do not be unbelieving, but believing." And Thomas answered and said to Him, "My Lord and my God!" Jesus said to him, "Thomas, because you have seen Me, you have believed. Blessed are those who have not seen and yet have believed."*
>
> *—John 20:27-29 (NKJV)*

Consider the scripture above and answer the following questions:

Why do you think Thomas didn't believe the other disciples' accounts of having seen Jesus?

___

___

___

___

___

How is Thomas's response before and after seeing the resurrected Christ similar to how people deal with doubt today?

___

___

___

___

___

What purpose might there have been in Thomas's missing the first appearance of Jesus?

___

___

___

___

What scars do you have to show from your experiences?

___

How do they work redemptively in your and other people's lives?

___

How is it is valuable to know that the damages we incur one moment can become the scars that point to a great and amazing God down the line?

___

How would you feel if God used your freedom to help someone else find theirs? How would knowing that could happen change the way you view your stuck-ness?

___

CHAPTER 6

GENERATIONS OF FREEDOM

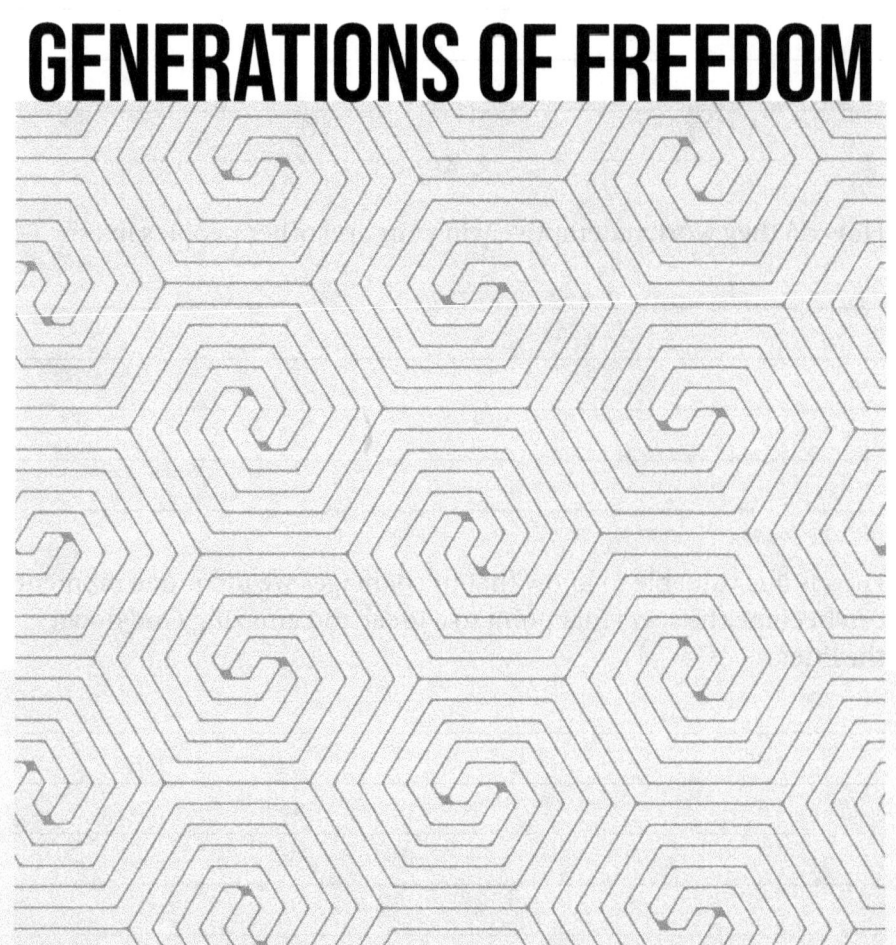

*If you quit, you're going to stay stuck.
However, if you push through, it's going to
be difficult. Which will you choose?*

As you read Chapter 6: "Generations of Freedom" in *Unstuck*, review, reflect on, and respond to the text by answering the following questions.

REVIEW, REFLECT, AND RESPOND:

In what area of people's lives do they find that there is always "one more time"?

_____
_____
_____

How does giving in "one more time" affect them and those they love?

_____
_____
_____

In what area of *your* life do you find there is always "one more time"?

_____
_____
_____

How does giving in "one more time" affect *you* and those you love?

_____
_____
_____

What is the origin of your one-more-time behavior—family, friends, etc.?

_____
_____
_____

What does it mean to be "free from your old life of sin . . . made into a new creation"?

_____
_____
_____

What do you think is significant about Jesus saying, "He who endures to the end will be saved," twice in the book of Matthew?

_____
_____
_____

What does it mean to endure? What does that look like in your life?

_____
_____
_____

What hope do you find in the fact that you cannot be a conqueror without something to overcome? What does that reveal to you about Paul's understanding of life on earth?

_____
_____
_____

How would you encourage someone who is disappointed in him or herself because they feel like they didn't persevere? They feel like they've already given up, or they're tempted to?

_____
_____
_____

> *Therefore, since we are surrounded by such a huge crowd of witnesses to the life of faith, let us strip off every weight that slows us down, especially the sin that so easily trips us up. And let us run with endurance the race God has set before us.*
>
> —*Hebrews 12:1 (NLT)*

Consider the scripture above and answer the following questions:

Who do you think is in that "huge crowd of witnesses" the writer to the Hebrews is talking about?

___

___

___

___

___

What were some of the sins that tripped them up? What trips you up?

___

___

___

___

How did they throw off those sins? How can you throw off the sins that are robbing you of peace and joy as you run with endurance?

___

___

___

___

___

CHAPTER 7

OUT OF YOUR CONTROL

You may feel trapped right now by circumstances outside of your control, but it is time to encourage yourself in the Lord and look for how He wants to restore you.

As you read Chapter 7: "Out of Your Control" in Unstuck, *review, reflect on, and respond to the text by answering the following questions.*

REVIEW, REFLECT, AND RESPOND:

What parts of your stuck-ness are outside of your control?

_____
_____
_____
_____

Like David, how do you strengthen yourself "in the Lord"?

_____
_____
_____
_____

In what ways have you found Pastor Richard's sentiments—"My point is that finding strength in the Lord is not a formula. There's not a single thing guaranteed to work every time you're stuck"—to be true?

_____
_____
_____
_____

How are you beginning to see that "It's not about a system—it's about a Person. It's about God, Himself, not how you get to Him"?

_____
_____
_____

> *Leave your native country, your relatives, and your father's family, and go to the land that I will show you. I will make you into a great nation. I will bless you and make you famous, and you will be a blessing to others. I will bless those who bless you and curse those who treat you with contempt. All the families on earth will be blessed through you.*
>
> —*Genesis 12:1-3 (NLT)*

Consider the scripture above and answer the following questions:

From your perspective, what was risky about God's instructions to Abraham?

_____
_____
_____
_____

What comfort do people find in the familiar?

_____
_____
_____
_____

Looking at where you are right now, what might the Lord be telling you to leave—fear, grief, security?

_____
_____
_____
_____

You wrote earlier which parts of your stuck-ness were *outside* of your control. Which parts of your stuck-ness are within your control? How can you own them?

_____
_____
_____
_____

Why is owning your behavior the first step toward freedom?

_____
_____
_____
_____

Spiritually speaking, where is the Lord asking you to go?

_____
_____
_____
_____

What is holding you in the place where you are?

_____
_____
_____

How can a person know if he or she is exactly where the Lord wants them?

_____
_____
_____

CHAPTER 8

WHERE ARE YOU?

If you're overthinking how stuck you are, you aren't going to be looking at the solution— your focus is going to stay on the problem.

As you read Chapter 8: "Where Are You?" in Unstuck, review, reflect on, and respond to the text by answering the following questions.

REVIEW, REFLECT, AND RESPOND:

Are you more likely to look within or without when it comes to "blame"?

_____
_____
_____
_____
_____

Pastor Richard instructs: "I want you to take a few moments to do some soul searching. Don't think of excuses or the lies we tell ourselves to feel better, and don't just say, 'It's all my fault.' Instead, honestly, sit back and evaluate; ask God for clarity." Where are you right now?

_____
_____
_____
_____
_____
_____

How did you get where you are?

_____
_____
_____
_____
_____

> *For everything there is a season, a time for every activity under heaven. A time to be born and a time to die. A time to plant and a time to harvest.*
>
> —*Ecclesiastes 3:1-2 (NLT)*

Consider the scripture above and answer the following questions:

What wisdom do you see in this chapter's Bible verses?

_____
_____
_____
_____
_____
_____

What "time" do you feel like you're in?

_____
_____
_____
_____
_____

How have you found it easy or hard to put your hope in God Himself instead of change?

_____
_____
_____
_____
_____
_____

For what might you need to forgive yourself? How easy do your find forgiving yourself? Why?

_____
_____
_____
_____

What does it mean that "God is not problem-oriented"? What kind of oriented is He?

_____
_____
_____
_____

What would it look like for you to "quit fighting and start resting"?

_____
_____
_____
_____

In deciding which route to take—fighting or resting—how confident are you that you could clearly hear the Holy Spirit regarding what He wants you to do?

_____
_____
_____
_____

What is the possibility that your instance of being stuck is really a forced Sabbath?

_____
_____
_____
_____

Is your natural inclination to follow the cycles and rhythms of your body or ignore them and push through for the sake of productivity? How can you tell?

_____
_____
_____
_____

Answer the big questions God might have for you:

- Where are you?

    _____
    _____

- Who told you you're stuck?

    _____
    _____

How can you embrace this time when you feel you're stuck, so you can get everything out of it that God wants for you?

_____
_____
_____
_____

CHAPTER 9

SUPERNATURAL, NOT SUPERHUMAN

Wherever you are, you can be supernatural in that setting, from working in a factory to crunching numbers in an office to wiping snotty noses at home.

As you read Chapter 9: "Not Superhuman, Supernatural" in *Unstuck*, review, reflect on, and respond to the text by answering the following questions.

REVIEW, REFLECT, AND RESPOND:

What is your gut reaction when people talk to you about having "heard from God"? Why do you think you feel this way?

_____
_____
_____
_____
_____
_____

How does God talk to His people?

_____
_____
_____
_____
_____
_____

What do you think Pastor Richard meant when he said, "God designed our lives to be more than just natural; He created us to also operate in the supernatural"?

_____
_____
_____
_____
_____
_____

> *"Most assuredly, I say to you, he who believes in Me, the works that I do he will do also; and **greater** works than these he will do because I go to My Father."*
>
> —*John 14:12-14 (NKJV, author emphasis)*

Consider the scripture above and answer the following questions:

What *works* did Jesus do that He is referring to in this chapter's verses?

_____
_____
_____
_____

How is it possible that simply by going to His Father, Jesus provided the way for believers to do *greater works*?

_____
_____
_____
_____

Considering that Jesus was *one person* who walked on the earth for only *thirty-three years* during which time He focused on *twelve disciples*, in what ways could the works that believers have accomplished since He went to the Father be "greater" than the ones He Himself performed in his earthly body?

_____
_____
_____
_____

What role does the Holy Spirit play in your life?

_____
_____
_____
_____
_____

In what ways would you like the Holy Spirit to be more active in your life?

_____
_____
_____
_____
_____

What does "being in ministry" mean to you?

_____
_____
_____
_____
_____

How would you differentiate between clergy and laypeople? How much of your understanding is based on misconceptions?

_____
_____
_____
_____
_____

"If you're a follower of Christ Jesus . . . you're just trying to be the best version of yourself that you can be, with Jesus' help and power within you to accomplish God's plan for you on this planet." How daunting would it be for you to make that statement your "ministry"?

_____
_____
_____
_____

If you embraced that idea of ministry, how could you show the Light of the World and be a bearer of hope in a way that allows those in darkness to approach you?

_____
_____
_____
_____

From what sources of power do you need to disconnect, so you can connect with the true source of power—the Holy Spirit?

_____
_____
_____
_____

CHAPTER 10

TUNE IN

How do you hear a whisper in a loud environment? You must listen carefully. You have to tune in; otherwise, a whisper will be easy to miss.

As you read Chapter 10: "Tune In" in *Unstuck*, review, reflect on, and respond to the text by answering the following questions.

REVIEW, REFLECT, AND RESPOND:

From where and how do people get their information in today's world?

_____

_____

_____

_____

What are you most consistently "tuned in" to? How does that source of information or method of communication influence your ability to hear from God?

_____

_____

_____

_____

_____

How would you respond or have you responded to the myriad explanations people give for not hearing God: He's too hard to find . . . The Bible is too cryptic . . . God only talks to a special few . . . etc.?

_____

_____

_____

_____

_____

What would you do to troubleshoot with someone who is concerned that he or she is not hearing from God?

___

How can you tell when other voices are drowning out God's voice?

___

What do you do to quiet the other voices, so you can hear from God?

___

In what ways has God shown that He's listening to you and wants you to have free two-way communication with Him?

___

Pastor Richard grabs his notebook, sits on the floor, and writes out his questions for God. What method have you found is most effective for keeping track of God's and your conversations?

___

> *And behold, the Lord passed by, and a great and strong wind tore into the mountains and broke the rocks in pieces before the Lord, but the Lord was not in the wind; and after the wind an earthquake, but the Lord was not in the earthquake; and after the earthquake a fire, but the Lord was not in the fire; and after the fire a still small voice.*
>
> —1 Kings 19:11-12 (NKJV)

Consider the scripture above and answer the following questions:

In your experience, has God revealed Himself in the wind, the earthquake, and the fire or the still small voice? What has that looked like in real life?

_____

_____

_____

_____

In which method are you most likely to hear Him? What does that method say about you and the way you give and receive communication?

_____

_____

_____

_____

What does God speaking in a still small voice—when He's capable of much, much more—reveal about His character?

_____

_____

_____

_____

CHAPTER 11

DISCERNING HIS VOICE

Father God wants you to spend enough time in His presence to know Him, so when all the voices of this world are competing for your attention, you'll be able to pick His out from the crowd.

As you read Chapter 11: "Discerning His Voice" in *Unstuck*, review, reflect on, and respond to the text by answering the following questions.

REVIEW, REFLECT, AND RESPOND:

What does the enemy sound like in your life? What does he say? What means of communication does he use?

_____
_____
_____
_____
_____
_____

In your opinion or experience, what is the difference between "tuning in" to God and recognizing and responding to His voice?

_____
_____
_____
_____
_____
_____

How do you distinguish between all the voices competing for your attention?

_____
_____
_____
_____
_____
_____

> "You fathers—if your children ask for a fish, do you give them a snake instead? Or if they ask for an egg, do you give them a scorpion? Of course not! So if you sinful people know how to give good gifts to your children, how much more will your heavenly Father give the Holy Spirit to those who ask him."
>
> —Luke 11:11-13 (NLT)

Consider the scripture above and answer the following questions:

What challenges do you face when it comes to viewing God as your good, good Father?

_____
_____
_____
_____
_____

How has your view of Him changed depending on your season of life?

_____
_____
_____
_____
_____

Parallel to the good gifts earthly fathers give to their children, Jesus said your heavenly Father will give the Holy Spirit. How do these gifts compare?

_____
_____
_____
_____

With which of the enemy's abuses of Scripture are you familiar? What do they sound like?

- Pretzel Logic

    _____
    _____
    _____

- Condemnation

    _____
    _____
    _____

In what ways has the Holy Spirit changed the Bible from words on a page talking about God into a Spirit-breathed, life-giving way of connecting with God intimately and personally?

_____
_____
_____

In what instances have you seen believers not receive what they need from God because their view of Him or their unbelief limits what they can receive from Him?

_____
_____
_____

Pastor Richard lists times of crisis, benefits for another person, and redemptive purposes as to why God needs us to hear from Him. Why do you think He needs you to hear from Him?

_____
_____
_____

What "haptics" does God employ to get your attention?

_____

_____

_____

_____

When have you seen yourself or someone else be a bearer of collateral grace? How did others benefit from it?

_____

_____

_____

_____

How might considering your current stuck-ness as a means to bless others through collateral grace change your perspective toward it?

_____

_____

_____

CHAPTER 12

THAT OR BETTER

God wants you to trust that the desires that He puts in your heart will be more ultimately fulfilling than anything you can cook up on your own.

As you read Chapter 12: "That or Better" in *Unstuck*, review, reflect on, and respond to the text by answering the following questions.

REFLECT AND TAKE ACTION:

Is your natural inclination to feel hopeful or hopeless when you face obstacles? How does that manifest in your thoughts and words?

_____
_____
_____

Pastor Richard said, "Sometimes God shows you something, but that's not 'it'—it's just a way of getting you to trust, to take a step." How does God work with your heart to keep you looking to Him as your source of hope?

_____
_____
_____

When has what you were picturing for yourself not been as good as God's best for you?

_____
_____
_____
_____

Describe the principle of That or Better in your own words. How would you use it to encourage someone whose hope is flagging?

_____
_____
_____
_____

When have you seen Interest give you—or someone else—entrance?

_____
_____
_____

Who have you seen embrace the belief that "God is in it all"? How did they act as ambassadors allowing God to reach through them into any and every dream He has for His kids?

_____
_____
_____

Conversely, who have you seen who was so focused on getting unstuck that they missed the point that God's dreams were bigger for them than just getting out of their situation?

_____
_____
_____

How possible is that what looks stuck only looks that way because of a person's limited perspective and vision? What can people do to widen their view of their stuck-ness?

_____
_____
_____

Even if you feel that being stuck is your own fault, what hope can you cultivate believing that God is not disappointed in you, and His promises cannot be thwarted?

_____
_____
_____

> *These were the true heroes, commended for their faith, yet they lived in hope without receiving the fullness of what was promised them. But now God has invited us to live in something better than what they had—faith's fullness! This is so that they could be brought to finished perfection alongside of us.*
>
> — *Hebrews 11:39-40 (TPT)*

Consider the scripture above and answer the following questions:

When have you had to "shake off the selfish idea that it is all about you"?

_____
_____
_____
_____

How does reading about the true heroes in the Bible who did not receive the fullness of God's promises to them in their lifetimes encourage you?

_____
_____
_____
_____
_____

Look back at your list of dashed hopes and broken dreams from chapter 1. (If you didn't write that list, do it now.) What do you feel about those deferred hopes now? Any changes?

_____
_____
_____
_____

CHAPTER 13

SHOW THEM HOW TO BE FREE

What better way to serve others than to show them how to be free?

As you read Chapter 13: "Show Them How to Be Free" in *Unstuck*, review, reflect on, and respond to the text by answering the following questions.

REFLECT AND TAKE ACTION:

In this last chapter, Pastor Richard asks a poignant question: "What's your motive for getting unstuck?" If you're truthful, what is your motive?

_____
_____
_____
_____

How selfish is your motive? Who else stands to benefit from your getting unstuck?

_____
_____
_____
_____

How can looking beyond your own need actually help you bring freedom to someone else?

_____
_____
_____
_____

How does the story of Elijah and the widow flesh out the principle that even in our barest of circumstances, there is still *something* to give?

_____
_____
_____
_____

What might God be asking you to give, so He can give the same back to you?

_____
_____
_____
_____

What do you have—knowledge, passion, energy, etc.—that you can sow now in the hope of reaping when the time comes?

_____
_____
_____
_____

What mentality might still be holding you in slavery, similar to the Egyptian mentality that held the children of Israel captive between Pharaoh's army and the Red Sea?

_____
_____
_____
_____

How are you beginning to see that it's really not about a solution? It's about a relationship with a God who is willing and able to set you free?

_____
_____
_____

How possible is it that God's main goal is not to get people unstuck? It is to connect with His children in any way that gets their attention? Explain.

_____
_____
_____
_____

How can you use what you see—at any time—as stuck-ness to be a testimony to God's power to unstick you? What's stopping you from doing just that?

_____
_____
_____
_____

> *You're here to be light, bringing out the God-colors in the world. God is not a secret to be kept. . . . I'm putting you on a light stand. Now that I've put you there on a hilltop, on a light stand—shine! Keep open house; be generous with your lives. By opening up to others, you'll prompt people to open up with God, this generous Father in heaven.*
>
> —*Matthew 5:14-16 (MSG)*

Consider the scripture above and answer the following questions:

Has your witness brought out the God-colors in the world, or are you more likely to "beat people over the head with your Bible"?

_____
_____
_____
_____

How attractive is your life to lost, stuck people? What light are you shining?

_____
_____
_____
_____

What opportunities can you look for in order to be a light-giver? If you don't know, who can you ask to help you? Do it sooner than later!

_____
_____
_____
_____

www.ingramcontent.com/pod-product-compliance
Lightning Source LLC
Chambersburg PA
CBHW062121080426
42734CB00012B/2946